D0942494

Gloryland_____

Glory

Gloryland
and

Anne Marie Macari

ALICE JAMES BOOKS
FARMINGTON, MAINE

© 2005 by Anne Marie Macari
All rights reserved
Printed in the United States

10 9 8 7 6 5 4 3 2 1

Alice James Books are published by
Alice James Poetry Cooperative, Inc.,
an affiliate of the University of Maine at Farmington.

Alice James Books
238 Main Street
Farmington, ME 04938

www.alicejamesbooks.org

Library of Congress Cataloging-in-Publication Data
Macari, Anne Marie.
  Gloryland / Anne Marie Macari.
    p. cm.
  ISBN-13: 978-1-882295-50-0 (pbk.)
  ISBN-10: 1-882295-50-1 (pbk.)
  1. Motherhood—Poetry. 2. Body, Human—Poetry. I. Title.

PS3563.A2335G58 2005
811'.6—DC22
2005009738

Alice James Book gratefully acknowledges support from the University
of Maine at Farmington and the National Endowment for the Arts. ❦

Cover image: Detail of "Pregnant Woman Stretching" by Paul Matthews.

for my parents
Katherine and Joseph Macari

Also by Anne Marie Macari

Ivory Cradle

Contents

One

Acknowledgements_____

Grateful acknowledgement is made to the editors of the
following journals and anthologies, in which some of these
poems first appeared.

The American Poetry Review: "Abort," "As If the Body,"
  "Drenched," "Gloryland," "Madonna Enthroned,"
  "New York, 1927," "Radio," "Still Life with Magnolia
  and Dove"
The Bloomsbury Review: "Seed"
Five Points: "Annunciation," "Night Feeding," "Little
  Church," "Sunbathing," "Palace of Longing"
Gulf Coast: "Rose-bed"
The Iowa Review: "Child Resting on Her Desk," "Mary's
  Blood"
The Journal: "All the Earth Around"
Luna: "Sickness," "Snowfall"
Lyric: "The Accident"
The Massachusetts Review: "Elegy for a Girl Singer"
Prairie Schooner: "Stick of Light," "Blue Duck"
Provincetown Arts: "With Child"
Shenandoah: "Even Love," "Of All The Gods"
TriQuarterly: "Absence," "Cut Roses," "Have You Ever
  Started Your Life Over?"
Poetry Daily Anthology: "Even Love"

"New York, 1927" appeared in *Never Before: Poems About First Experiences*, edited by Laure-Anne Bosselaar and published by Four Way Books.

The author also wishes to thank the editors of *Five Points* for awarding her the James Dickey Prize for Poetry for the poems "Little Church," "Sunbathing," and "Palace of Longing."

One

Our journey had advanced—

Our feet had almost come

To that odd Fork in Being's Road—

—EMILY DICKINSON

Mary's Blood

It was Mary's blood made him, her blood
sieved through meaty placenta to feed him,
grow him, though Luke wrote she was no more
than the cup he was planted in, a virgin
no man ever pressed against or urged
who could barely catch eyes with the towering
angel but felt God come to her like light
through glass, like a fingerprint left on glass;
still, it's hard to believe she never wanted
to be rid of the thing inside her, wasn't
shamed carrying him, the child's
perfect head pointing at the ground
and rubbing her cervix like the round earth
rubbing the thin wall of the sky that holds it.
All women reach the time of wanting it out
but not wanting it out, not knowing
what's coming, so she must have spread
her legs in anguish because what was inside
pressing her membranes for release
was both herself and a stranger;
and she must have cried out
as the small head crowned,
splitting her, her pelvis swung
wide to push him through the wall
of this world, till what came from her
was a child lit with her own gore,
soiled, everything open so her inside
was now outside, cracked open, it means
mother to crack open, to be rent
by what comes to replace her. Such

is love—the only way. It was Mary's
blood made him: his eyes, tongue,
his penis, her milk fattened his legs,
made hair on the crown of his head,
she grew caul to wrap him and door
to come through and nothing, not even
crying *Father, Father,* to the warped
blue sky can change it.

New York, 1927

This time it's true, as much as I remember
from what she told me. How she gave birth
in their tenement and it took nearly two days.
In America she was Mary, always Mary,
all those hours begging her namesake
for help, the midwife muttering about
going home, thinking *this one's dead*, with
the baby wedged between her narrow hips,
a cross on the wall, her fingers gripping
the sheets. Years later I understood
what she meant. How she drifted
in and out, like being on a boat in fog,
rowing, drifting, but called away from
everyone she knew toward a wilderness.
As if she had to go out alone to meet
the child and bring him through not just
with her body, but some other part of her
searching at the same time. Of course
she prayed, she knew what it smelled like
to be that close to death and she wanted to live,
to get the baby out alive, her first-born
who unlocked her for the others.
In the next room her husband and his father
heard the child cry and could finally feel
their own sickness and fear overtaking them.
Maybe they'd been drinking, or maybe it was
her father-in-law's red hair startling her
as he came into the bedroom just when
a familiar darkness began refilling her belly.
His eyes looked wild with confusion for

his first grandson and though she knew
she was alive, he looked strange
to her as a being from the other world
and put his hands into his pockets and pulled
the cloth out so all his money fell—no
she said he threw it—onto her bed,
silver coins landing around her legs,
the white insides of his pockets flapping
out like tiny wings at his hips. He called in
all his sons—my stunned grandfather
and his unmarried brothers—and pointed
to my father sleeping on the bed all
washed and wrapped in white by
the midwife. *Now,* he told the men,
you work only for him.

Night Feeding

It's hot snow dripping on the plain
of your stomach, the child's desperate mouth
rooting till you rub your breast
against his cheek to orient him.
All night long he wakes every two hours
and his sucking tows you inside yourself,
tugs you beneath the muscles of your face
and neck and into the muscle of your heart.
You are all water, all milk, from the soup
of the pelvis to your wet eyes,
you are sour desire thrumming, the cord
he pulls reaching into your ankle,
you feel it there, it travels up
the inside of your leg, travels
to the nipple itself as you
release and empty yourself,
your back to the window where
the moon lulls the trees to sleep
and brushes your shoulders. It's all
more than you could have hoped. To be
so alone with him, so undone
by exhaustion, gazing at what
you made—at the cloudy drink that ebbs
in the corners of his mouth,
at the child staring back
with blue eyes; both of you
rocking outside of time toward
a milkless future, both of you
rocking and you trying not

to fall asleep, to have this hour
in its fullness, weeping breasts and
hungry baby and you still large
with creation, burning where
he left you ripped and bloody,
as if he'd dug his tunnel through you,
from nothing, dug his way here
where you sustain him with this
blue milk, this light, streaming.

Soup

When I made soup last night—vivid carrots,
pale leeks and potatoes, salt bursting in hot
water and the rose of garlic opening in
my hand—I sliced and chopped to break the silence
and with pestle and fire called up a pungent change.
My fingers split open the ghost-bird, plunged
it in the pot to make a broth of its soul,
its plucked wings floating near the top, and later
tossed its bones in the trash far from its home,
far from where its head had been crushed and used
for something, I don't know what. In the end I had
a rich, private brew on my stove, candles
burning, windows draped in steam, voices descending
the steps, my table laden with soup and bread.

Child Resting on Her Desk

When you lay your head on the desk
you hear a riot in the wood—air sucked

down a hollow hall and crows calling.
In that long passage built by sound

there's no sleep, only one door after another,
and noises threatening to burst in,

not into the world of the wooden desk with
its irregular heart-beat, but the world

of the room and its children. You hold
your head above the scarred plank

so that the clamor in the wood hardly
reaches you, so visions won't be afraid

to find you, your neck twisted and
your fist bunched under your hair,

you can't say what's coming, something
beyond milk, something your left hand

curled into position and etching out
its first sounds can't hear yet—biting

your cheek, the smell of the pencil
still on your fingers. And while you try

to ignore the scuffing feet under the desks,
you see that part of you is not a child at all,

part of you is something besides a person,
a floating blanket above your child's

cramped body, still waiting even when
the teacher claps her hands to revive

the class so when you lift your head
the blanketing-self brushes your face,

you are waiting to become, you'll wait as long
as you have to, shell to feather, ink to utterance,

body beyond the body, beyond
the body, pulling you, clumsy and tripping,

leading you through membranes of self,
filmy home you can't see like inside

the leafy head of a huge tree
you keep climbing, branch after branch,

twigs somehow keeping you aloft,
and how you learn to step on them without

looking, as if you really knew the way.

No Prophecy

The statue of Mary keels side to side
carried up to her mother's church, St. Anne's,
on the shoulders of the faithful.
Who wants to be a statue? Who wants to be
anything but flesh, or leaves, or
the sock of evening coming down across
the trees to smother the daylight?
Shouldn't what happened be enough?
Without angels or stars, no prophecy,
no miracles with Mary attended
by messengers from above, never free
or alone, never far from the gaze of
a stony apostle? Even now the bell
in her chest wants to ring and she goes back
to a moment, lost, a last morning, bathing,
bending over a bucket, her belly
huge and taut, crisscrossed with blue veins—
heavenly body, swollen breasts, aching back, holy,
holy in the flesh and the burning, in the cord
and mouth, holy tongue, lips, nipples,
water dripping down her legs—holy, holy.

As If the Body

In the alleys below her heart,
a drain, blood gathering
in a pool, a cistern.

When it overflows, first just
a drip, then a stream
hidden, the way spirits
hide inside trees and rocks,

there in that well, teacup
inside flesh, is a crouching thing,
how it claws when it's flushed
from her, how each time

there's a tug so strong, aching
sacrum and arch drawing
toward her thighs.

Then she's a long root
of blood, as if the body, as if
the body, as if—no,
of course not—something tips
over inside her.

Annunciation

When I asked her how the world began
my mother's face went blank.

I was very young, trying for the first time
to see the universe as endless.

All I saw was darkness swirling into itself.
How could anything be endless?

But how could it be contained? By what? All cosmos
held in the crook of an elbow?

There were no answers, though I thought the clouds
were great wings trying

to help me, and thought my blood changed
directions. What could I be

but an echo? Stranded here while the universe
grows like a belly dense

with stars. And I thought we were all orbiting inside
that belly, and light could pass

through me but I wouldn't feel it. Years later, ·
my son told me how

he was conceived. He said he stood in a cloud
and pointed at me: *I want her,*

then put down his bow and arrow and came
when my back was turned

and entered through my shoulder blades.
What I don't know

is everything: stars, sand, salt, dust,
molecules and atoms,

and how they come scudding through the door
full of news from distances

I can't imagine. Some day I'll tell my sons
the truth, that I knew

they were coming. Nothing I could see or even
feel but a sense sometimes

that I was permeable, the cells inside me
gathering and spreading.

I hate to think of galaxy after galaxy. All matter
burning up and shucked off.

The endless signs of demise and change.
I still can't grasp

how anything at all can exist and what made
the maker. And sometimes I'm choked

with love and forget my own ignorance.
Maybe just at that moment

light is pressing through a tree and reaching
my window, and I am

satisfied, joyful, though I know there's
nothing there, just light,

announcing itself, coming through.

With Child

Stretched and weighed down, as if
in a hundred pockets of self

she had crammed her calcified
secrets and regrets,

the minerals of things never said.
So much longs

to be filled, down to the spaces
between bones,

cavities and caves in her head, and for years
the slack uterus.

Till finally the self
is too solid, bursting,

her legs rooted, her head tilted toward
the light. Crossing

the street, the new life turned inside,
pressing down,

pulling its taut rope. She gasped in pain

wanting to squat and rock
herself free while

the false gods of alchemy rushed by
in their gold taxis

and one called out *it's a boy*, which
is all they ever said.

A child in swirling brine, distorting her,
crushing her organs.

She headed for something
tall and strong to lean on, alone inside

her hundred cocoons,
her private spinning,

her silk veils and blood-soaked

membranes. The crowd passed by
as the infant

continued his lessons, her spine
lined up against

the tree, his spine curled inside.
Soon he would arrive

leaving the invisible grown beyond
proportion,

with only a trace of him left, a trail
of phosphorous in

her own dark sea.

Palace of Longing

How many minute doors
in the body? Valves and
pinched places. Eyelids,
the many drums. And did

the artist think of them when
he painted the corpse, bent
over like a mourner,
his face, color of the strange

sky above? I'm all
mixed up, lost in this
last room of the exhibit
the painting on the wall

so large that the exit door
looks like a mouse hole,
and the shuffling feet seem
to come from inside me.

And painted near an angel's
wing is the artist himself
looking so much like the man
I loved so long who

didn't in return, humbled
above the dead man, yet
larger than he should be,
as if he knew I'd be here

reading the captions, mute
and so close, still not painted
into the scene, remembering
when I wanted to be

the brush in his hand,
the pigment he ground.
In the hollow of my neck,
in the holes behind

my eyes, at all the gates
of being where I once
waited, a ghost haunting
myself, I finally passed

into myself, wanting
to live. In the painting
there's a woman behind
the artist, her weeping face

half-covered. I don't know
how I stopped leaning
into his absence, how I
stepped through the door—

left the palace of longing—
hands unclenched, even
the wild crown
of the head

dilated.

Absence

Talking to the children's absence, you imagine them
canoeing or sitting before a fire, sparks

arcing like imitation stars. There's so much to say,
even in the unrelenting heat, the sun

balanced overhead while you collect facts for them
as if they can hear you: how the barracuda's jaw

can spread so wide then thrash and rip into anything,
how bees can't find their hive if it's moved

more than a few inches, how your own house settles
fraction by fraction into clay and river stone,

and dust is alive though you sweep it into piles
meaning the desert is a guest in the corner

of your room, meaning your feet keep stirring clouds
of creatures and you pass over animal and plant

and never feel the burden, or do feel the burden and bend
like a sapling, like a heavy flower brushing

the ground. This is what separation trains you for.
You as an envelope releasing them, you ripping

the cord, you with your stains on them, the ones
you need ten hundred mirrors

to see. The old goddess of tether and straw, the one
who makes you to lie down, to be crushed

till you come out oil of fish, oil of granite, come out
ash and live in the fine grit under their feet,

who licked you alive and left the taste in your own mouth,
your own love: sand, ground tooth, spider,

sawdust, hair, and adoration turned to powder,
and absence teaching its teaching and all

you cannot say, you'll never say, swallowed, a coating
inside lungs and all passageways, all orifices being

the openings of absence, and what you want to say turns
to air, but you try your prayer once more: old goddess

of rain, wash us with your silent tongue as if
we were always being born, just born, slick

and stunned, with our legs kicking

Abort

That sound of ice gripping the river, cold
infecting things, was the sound of my grandmother

confessing to my mother in a sudden,
cracked way, her voice getting so far ahead

she could only follow, shaking and shocked.
How could I have guessed, as proper as

she was, as prim, who never said anything
except through blue eyes? After sixty years

that upstate New York freezing winter
still in her throat, trying to escape—

husband out of work, one sick child, and more
than cold that northern dread above them,

the sky snow-fed and engorged, her shame
in their small bed questioning how

to undo what had been done. Think of
that lineage of blank looks,

women in my family who said *no, not now*—
as I did once, grieving for

the night sky of my belly. Sometimes I hear
a clamor of blame, boats coming

to harbor in my arms. So much pushing, pulling,
smacking, sucking, a woman

sanctified by kisses and fists. And still I try
to say yes all my days, as she did, but

the joining of beings is so hard, some days
I'm far away, locked in my skin,

unable, like her, to speak. I only want then
the emptiness of my night sky,

the blackness of my belly
for comfort. I think I need

to practice being alone, long before
they all leave—before the day

I too am snatched, a large being aborted:
my thin hair, tired brown eyes,

my nails, heart, closing throat,
swollen ankles; unjoined

and joining, saying *no, not now,* then *yes, yes.*

Horseshoe Crabs

for Jeremy

Their bodies float to shore and he dashes
to collect them, upending them to dry,
all their feet walking the wind.
They'll be forgotten before they're dusty

and brittle on his shelf, like the seashells
scattered in drawers, or deer bones he found,
or pinned to cardboard some sad, papery moths:
his room of stunned beings and their rot.

Not to mention, pocketknives, belt buckles,
pennies. Sometimes I think he came not
from me but from nothing, then like fire
meeting air he flared up. Walking on his knees

in sand he's taking in elements one by one,
not yet knowing there's one he can't name
or even collect, though he keeps trying.
Rising out of water, staring through

the golden crab's shield, he won't find what
he's looking for, though the pleasure of it will
move him to search in blood and rock,
microscope, telescope, water, paper and prayer,

but see—whatever's lined up on his shelf—
it's not there.

In the Kingdom of Cloth

I'm ironing my son's shirt with its man-sized
collar and buttons pulling

from fabric, no easy way out while the kitchen
whispers, no respite from

coffee pot or limp plants. On the porch
my youngest tries to trance

chickadees and greedy finches as I do
each sleeve in one

or two strokes. The shirt with its open arms,
its optimism. As if a woman

doesn't spill a bit of her own blood, knowing
how heat sears the open places,

how wounds heal like wrinkles nearly ironed out,
leaving fine traces

and tracks. I drape pressed shirts on chair-backs
as if invisible men

sit at my table, I fold mounds of pants and
socks before them. Outside,

my son stares at clouds while I rest the hissing
iron with its small holes,

its pointy nose for getting under arms and
around shoulders, for making

creases relax and the blue cotton crisp again—
small mercies in

the kingdom of cloth, where animals are made
bare of feathers and fur,

and fields gleaned of infant clouds, where looms
rise, moaning, and seams,

one after the other, are straightened and joined
and so on without end, all

the cracked hands that hold them rubbed by rivers
of thread and stained with dye,

where hovels or mansions are sewn over flesh,
and children make buttons

of bone and shell. See my table littered with spoils,
hear my son cry out,

waving his arms like flags so the frightened
birds burst off the feeder, leaving

gashes and echoes in the serge-blue sky.

Snowfall

This snow becomes all snow, even from other
times or cities I've never seen—Berlin
or Budapest—a graveyard of snow burying
centuries, a garden of revelation where
the living and dead stare at the same white sky
for thousands of years. My face becomes
a white mask, the yard a bed of moths,
cold and stiff, garden of crystals, stars frost-fired,
flowers frozen, their ice-tongues hanging.
A past without color, stirred by snow it
arises out of awakening and sleep,
breaking memory, smelling of nothing except
childhood, broom-swept memory, warm house, the sky
choking: cloud-world, changed world, covered and cold.

The Accident

Even if no one's hurt, it's the nearness,
the knowledge that's painful, the 66
memories, the sudden partings like
my aunt when blood burst in her brain
and she fell in the crack
between worlds. A man knocks on
my window, and my sons seem far away,
cut off, though they reassure me and I see
their moving mouths and hear them
speaking and think this is nothing next
to other things so terrible to think of—
pictures I've seen, stories I've heard,
things that shouldn't be—I think
I couldn't put my dry lips to the dirt
hard enough to make up for it,
I couldn't kiss God the grub in the earth
long enough to atone for what's
broken, what might have broken,
what will surely one day break, though
the grub eyes could be long blue holes
of tenderness and stare back at me
as if saying that everything now
broken will again be whole, if that's
any help, if I can believe it.

Stick of Light

I looked for a stick of light that could pierce my heart—
maybe the spine of a young tree that I'd strip
of hair and branches. Maybe a flower blade,
its petal a bit of flesh glorified,
a boat dragged by light's undertow. Though no one
can hold such a stick, and no one can aim it
at her own heart, or die with light singeing
her hands. But only fall and breathe ashes,
only dig in the silky roots and hope
for the mocking flower-heads to return,
green horns first, then buds sealed and beating, as I
circle like a wasp wearing my thorn, stabbing
at air, wanting a splinter of light, hot and blue—
sliver, spear—because it's time now to draw blood.

Still Life with Magnolia and Dove

She says she wants to leave except her bones
are dissolving in her back so she can't

even walk; I know she's not writing
these phone numbers down.

It's her own story, I have no business,
but when she says *I haven't*

told anyone, I move the receiver
from my ear, already knowing

what she'll say as she describes her husband's
forearm-block-of-wood slamming

her head while outside the magnolia opens
flower by flower, each branch

bouncing when the petals spring apart.

Near my window, the dove turns toward
the sun and the pink streak

on its neck surprises me, I'm touched from all
angles by pink radiation—

heartsick. And just because I once thought
I'd die, it's not the same. If I ate

my own cocoon to get out, swallowed my fetid
corset till I stank of newness,

why should she care, trapped in her bed, dreaming
of dying, sky pouring

over the tree and the tree still opening.
Maybe in time the lost iris

of the eyes of Solomon will pluck our orbs
from their delirious cradles,

or maybe we need a madness we can cling to.
What we learn is never learned

enough, which I know when every window in my body
hurts to be opened and when I have said

too much. What I learn is never learned
enough no matter how close I sleep

to the sky, no matter what bird bends over me.
It's taken my whole life to get here,

a kind of safety she'll have to find somewhere
in the cup of occipital bone.

She cannot see my bird scratching the dirt, the flowers
breaking apart in the light,

she has her own story, she's living to tell it.

September

The hornets' uprising made a shadow over
the lawn and past the windows. So much streamed
by in that second she could hear an out-
of-tune harp bending air; leaves tearing branches,
the trees' fists grasping. Oh, almost no one
really saw a thing, though something was now
remade. She sat on the edge of the bed,
the clouds distant and silent. The room filled with
the yellow heart-beat of change. She slipped off
her shoes. On the nightstand the sunflower dropped
a thick coat of pollen onto its wide
green leaf, such gold, such a small world, it was powdered
light, a potion for sleep or love or else
something drastic, she didn't yet know which.

Blue Duck

The duck's head is so blue rising out of
its black neck—as though something's
hidden in its night-head deeper than the worms
of its mind. Of all the doors to walk through,
or dive through, it's this one, this pure center
of water circling and ringing where its beak
siphons and its body twists to find green
bread; duck of right-now passing along
the canal saying there's another door
altogether, a vastness to step into,
try to see yourself there, as if your heart
wore these deep blue feathers, as if
it pumped out its blood
into that white opening sky.

Have You Ever Started
Your Life Over?

If today she comes out of sleep, out of the story
where her tongue grows back and her eyelids unfold
like petals till the light is brilliant as two suns shining,

or if she awakens to children waiting for her to drive
to school, the hundred-year dishes in the sink,
sewing box open, a jar of buttons, the bloody needle
where she left it,
                              or if having stiffened into a doll
of sleep, porcelain face, painted lips, she is touched
into her life and must climb out of fossilized dreams
to find herself twisted in hair and sheets, buried in brambles,

                        if she's been poisoned by love

if she means for this day to be different and so has
covered her shrines with a sheet, while the children laugh,
such laughter! like another life she could still have

if she awakens to it, pours boiling water on the dishes,
grinds the coffee beans,

                        if she finally understands
that no one is coming to wake her, it's over, that waiting,
that longing, beauty's over, no one's watching, no one
cares whether she wakes up after all this time and it's only
light reaching through the curtains, touching her so she
      stirs in her white gown,
sweaty, still tired, but wanting to tear out of sleep's

womb into the plume of sun and its mesh of dust, to shake away
sleep's gauze, her limbs stiff as if newly grafted, mouth dry,

                    if she has to keep waking, a woman
undressing in a constant state of peeling dreams
away from her eyes

                    if she no longer imagines wars
being fought that she might sleep another hundred years,
the planes droning above as if for her sake,

                    but instead sits up in bed, feet
on the cold floor, and opens her eyes to the room with
its piles of books, clothes, lethargy and lust,
as if all that matters is to stand up, swallow the sour
debris of her mouth, stand up, no one's there,
stand up, walk to the sink, open the faucet, drink

Two

But we don't even know if Paradise
is behind or ahead of us.

—Fanny Howe

Book One

Light *was* being, held by her own hands or
touched like water burning bare skin.
In the beginning meant learning to see: a thousand
kinds of green, the vine-crawl along rocks,
the groping mouths of flowers. In the beginning
all they knew was yes, so when the first *no*
settled quietly around the tree
they thought it birdsong, it took days or weeks
for them to even notice its echo
in the leaves, an absence really, the start of loss.
Later, when the suffering began, who could
she turn to and say: *I didn't ask to be born*,
squatting, the light separate and cold, distant
as God, and she, already, refusing to kneel.

Madonna Enthroned

I find a stool so small it must be a child's
and lift it for her to see. Cracked paint
around her lips, around her peaceful eyes.
No wonder they find her weeping
in Astoria or Birmingham and lean a vial
to catch her tears while swarms of prayers
keep her stung and bleeding for all time. I tilt
the stool so she can see its short legs,
she knows I'm ashamed of how she's dressed:
crown, encrusted jewels, one patron after another
seeking favors. Madonna of the plate,
Madonna of the saucer. Sometimes the baby
Jesus stands on her lap fully formed like
a miniature lover, her one joy, sometimes
her hand rests on her swollen belly,
or she sits so stiff on her throne, so lost
and far away there's no talking to her.
Madonna of mud, of chickens and straw,
of girls like unopened packages.
So quiet I want to kiss the peach varnish
on her lips. Instead I pull out my knife
to scrape away the paint of her robe,
stripping the blue lapis that drapes
her shoulders and arms, flaking gold trim
into a plastic bag. Careful as I am it takes
time to get down to the stained linen bed
she's painted to, then to remake the robe
into a rainless sky and the gold into bright
hen feathers, Madonna enthroned with just
a rag now for modesty and that half-smile

that says nothing except *peace be with you*
or *have a nice day*, or *how did I get here*,
like a stamp on all the paintings, no defiance,
a bit stooped, a bit frozen for all time, though
I call her beautiful, wish I were that good, so
loving I could bear a god and not explode
with his light, and never double over with hate
for man or maker, never consider poison
an option, or wrist slashing, or sit on a window ledge
as if it were a throne or think if I jumped
I'd enter a blue world that would sponge
away sadness, loneliness, and that he wants
me like her, each molecule unresisting, so he
will take me then take me away if only I be
perfect and lo I will not blink, and lo
I will abide and know that all is right
and will be and is right; and I study the stool
because the throne's too big, she wants it closer
to the ground till she's almost squatting in dirt,
she wants to be everything, grit and flesh
and atmosphere, and yes, she's speaking to me,
says drink the world, the whole world, whispering,
this is my body given to you: flies around
the unhatched eggs, dogs, a child crying.

An Explanation for Galileo

*Pope Urban VIII ordered all the birds in his
gardens killed.*

—Dava Sobel, *Galileo's Daughter*

Some say it's grace to step one morning
into a Rome coated with

red light and begin killing lucifer's
smallest voices. I see

how it must have happened:
priests snapping the small

necks—sparrows, songbirds,
still shuddering in the grass.

I love the birds best, and after
all these years I believe more

in the orbiting planets, and that
everything swallowed

by dirt—feather and bone—
is sometimes sky, and sky

is sometimes dirt. But like
a child I want a story

where their broken necks
are twigs grafted to

the next world, so many
souls bursting from

the great tree of heaven.
Everyday I'm given another

garden for bowing and kneeling,
like this one, where birds

shriek and priests hurl eggs
from their nests, small oval worlds

falling through space, exploding on
the grass, a smattering of suns,

fragmented stars

The Man in the Garden

In the painting the birds have only one eye
and are almost bigger than the tree-tops
they perch in above the garden.

In my garden hidden birds know
when to sing or not, I think their lives
are like an eyelash fallen onto

a white page—and the man down
on his knees in the grass, planting
or crying, as if he's lost something there,

the birds point toward him for solace,
as if he's lost and will finally say so,
brought down by a beauty

only he sees, the walls around him
asleep, the trees nodding off.
And since anger is one of the six thousand

truths, then the sparrows and chickadees
must know it in the soft near-bone
of their fierce feathers. Though underneath

the dove's breast, bone has gone
to blood—and I too have stood
in the garden stripped to raw self

of no-anger and almost bled
onto the lumpy soil for in no-anger
it was hard to stand, and walking was strange,

but the sun still stood above us, the birds,
me, and the man in the painting, actually stars
were over him, and he wept.

Of All the Gods

It had something to do with touch. He was
my Moses, parting my sea of grief. I was
in the slick of it, underwater, half-drowned,
so when he spoke and touched my face I thought
I'd believe again if for once someone
entered my whole fish spine. I was born
from mud, I awoke. He came close to drink.
Eyes open. I saw for miles then, as if the walls
of the room were clouds parting; when you see the future
you should turn your head away, you should bow—my knees
wanted to sink but I stayed and stared back.
Of all the gods he was the one who listened,
listened with hands and mouth, calling me,
though I had yet to speak a single word.

Seed

After the wave there's the tide-pool in the ribbed
cup. Now I own what you left me and I'm
salt-rimmed, stained, lit by small hands trying
to feel their way inside, floating on the black
ocean beneath pelvic blood-stars. Because
I'm trying not to lose any, I sleep
against you to be the child on your back,
to be the fur on your skin, the eyes of your
shoulders. If I am the wolf drinking the milk
of darkness around your head, then you are
the lamb; or if I am the lamb then you are the wolf,
howling all night in my ear for the ordinary life.
I say to you: let your seed sprout from my lungs,
let me bear the strange animal of our love.

The Stolen Bible

for Jerry

He was restless, with his reverence askew,
saying prophets were thieves, that even truth
could be stolen: from someone's backpack, or
a clay jar in a cave, from a goat chewing
rotting parchment that's later passed through barbed wire
behind the backs of guards. This time it was
a cheap hotel where the room's sweet smell kept us
awake, he had to read *something*—the TV flashed
and King James bellowed from the nightstand—
and when he opened the drawer he heard the animals
of creation call to him—roosters, steamy sheep—
his eyes wild when he found the Book of Mormon
grinding its teeth. How many heavens could
one room hold? Shutting the TV, he walked
to the window and dropped the Mormon book
six floors down, all its angry angels falling
into shrubs, hovering and shrieking
over the pages splayed in dirt. He loved
inciting a skirmish, as if the light rain
were spit, contempt, the clouds in their old argument.
What did he care? Leaning out the window,
calling down to the bare garden, *Come*
unto me all ye that labour, tapping
his foot to the beat of *succor, succor.*
He closed the blinds and let the angels
fight it out and even as he packed
the cardboard Bible into his suitcase,
his burden was light and he slept the sleep
of the just. His mouth could have been full
of parchment and the stench of dust, he could have

recited in Hebrew or stood beneath the star-tree
reaching for the fruit. He could wait,
if he must, for the huge razor eye to blink—
that was his job—to steal the word of God
and cry it out, it was his one true purpose.

Elegy for a Girl Singer

My third secret was wanting to sing
in the voice of the chanteuse from a year
before I was born, to be a girl
whose beauty chimed in her mouth
and glistened her, the long throat
of song somehow born to be shaped
by her tongue and teeth while the waters
of saxophone rose around her. She had
a voice I'd follow anywhere, knowing
all the words, each song a story I needed.
They called them girl singers
but she knew husbands, hospitals, pills;
she knew the last husky song when the lungs
are no more than debris the music
left behind, some old love song
when the body's craving—the torch
of its emptiness—reveals a pelvic
atmosphere so vast no lover
will ever fill it, music skulking at
the body's doors, smoke in
the arteries or curled in the throat like
one last riff of black notes hooked
on the tongue. When she backs me
in my car I sing out, neck arched,
driving the extra miles just
to keep singing, till I'm erased
and she's just a note vibrating,
less than waterdrop or shadow,
till she's mounting the dash
and windshield, her note set

free, giving out breathsong
and agony, I mean dying,
I mean not one more chorus
unless you count memory,
a woman's voice lifting,
leaving her mouth one last time.

Rose-bed

It was only a morning vision, the voice almost my own,
the dream opening, roselike, so I could enter it
and I slept, then slept harder still, pulled by the weight
behind my eyes. For awhile I left behind
toast, coffee, the smells of our bed. Not moving
but heading toward the rose's center. I had one
hand on the door and began to enter, my in-
side body taken by the yellow heart,
pollen-dusted by the rose-bed, which could rock
me in any direction, it wouldn't matter which way
I went, or how I'd rise again to taste
my mouth that could not speak, though the voice
was almost my own and it comforted me, passing,
falling or rising, it didn't matter which.

Even Love

Green light came down from the heaven of
the jackals and crisscrossed the room where the bed
was slightly disturbed, sheets damp, curtains swaying,
curtains on which strange birds were painted, their wings
striped and half-opened, birds of paradise
with long tails like umbrellas. The moon-colored bed
that the bodies floated on was tender
as skin itself. Even love, in some way,
could be said to be wasteful, which was what
the jackals waited for. Tongues hanging,
covers already tearing where they lurked,
lamps overturned where they prowled for something spilled,
circling the bed, snapping at air and lace, foaming
over seed or blood on the pliant white sheet.

Cut Roses

Mornings I filled a simple glass for their thirst.
I don't know why they made me think of fish
or why their voices were muffled. They were waifs
of smoke and fire, getting close my eyes smarted,
they were inhabited, swimming here
from another garden and what I couldn't feel
they felt without effort, petals unfurling
where they held it all inside. I wished them a slow
and drawn out death. A long parting. Petal
at a time falling to my table. Finally, what
was left were eyes dried and bent over their yellowed
remains, discolored lids, useless now,
above them the bodiless brown eye with its stiff
lashes hanging from the brittle stem

and scanning the room with vigilance,
like the moving eyes of icons, how they step
from the painting, hang from the retina.
Of course the roses were dead, yellow roses
once stunning now just eyes out of their sockets,
I still smell them, drink my coffee before them
as we eye each other across the room.

Madame Sherri's House

If it was really a bordello, as the locals say,
why build in the woods, miles from nowhere?
And what's the crime in wearing feathers
or going naked under a fur coat?
There's something to be said for the feeling
of fur against skin, though the men who shot up
her house would have been shocked to find
their own wives or daughters washing dishes
with nothing on, just some silky thing
hanging open, the men sobbing over
their kitchen tables as if Columbus
had finally fallen off the edge of
the earth and there was no America
anymore, the woods thick again with green
ropes of hair, wide trees, heavy drops of light.

Sherri with her men, her costumes, her skin
moon-white as they disappeared into
the woods each summer with suitcases
of chocolate and champagne to her house
of bear rugs, porcelain, silver—it could
all be destroyed. A fire maybe.
I step over poison ivy, and though
it's forty years, lilies still blink on the pond
and scorched trees lean over the foundation.
See how dirt becomes us—mouse-ear, jewelweed,
milk of dandelion. Everything wild
creeping back. See naked Sherri lie down
with bind-weed and fleabane, a conflagration

in her bones, a flower blooming, burning,
falling underfoot, forgotten except for the sign
by the side of the road that points tourists
to the burned-down home of the whore.

Sickness

Wants even the snow in your eyes and the scab
above your lip from shaving. I saw it come
burning once, take a young man flat and keep him there
turning his legs all black while his heart kept

pumping for no good reason. I helped carry
my dying Nana to the bathroom and heard her cry
for her long dead mother and father. I kept
smiling and calm in the emergency room

when God was a machine beeping and the patient
a contortionist, it was once upon a time and sickness,
that jealous lover, was forcing electrical charges
through lips, and noises surfaced from

the underworld; the jealous lover didn't mind
who died or who was maimed as long as she
could possess, she called herself a god and so
could change shapes and go inside any way

she wanted and come out when she was good
and ready. I saw her burst alive like religion once
renounced, taking revenge till you and I were
believers again, bowing down and praising

all manner of horror, till the perfect self, the one
pumping blood and breathing, the one with
the lantern held high in the center of your chest,
was going blind and deaf. Who isn't waiting?

Who is right at this moment counting heartbeats
and trying to learn the secrets of love? Sick
isn't the word at all—*stricken, starving,
lost, broken, afflicted, betrayed—long*

winter, long winter. You can be *changed
and transposed* or one last time you can be
reprieved, returned, released—thinking,
didn't I walk through the valley of the shadow,

didn't my cup run over? How you longed for
goodness, for *god,* the way a child does,
memorizing the words, *mercy, forgiveness,*
and how for a moment you could forego

all jealousy and see yourself *whole, healed,*
no matter if one day we would all lose
everything, by the body denied, spit out,
catapulted into kingdom come.

Glass Beach

for Suzie

I'm no collector, I throw things out when I can,
      but I dragged my bag of muck

through surf and broke my back searching.
      The beach was just an old

bottle dump on an island, with tinted beds
      of glass like pieces

of a jagged ocean, aqua and green. Or with shards
      of dinner plates and brown

beer bottles. A friend brought me that I might
      lower myself and end up

scraping sand, and hear the ghosts of bottles
      clinking when waves hit,

see the sky as mosaic, fragments over us,
      scratched and smoky.

At sunset I climbed the hill above the beach
      and sat under ironwood trees

in coarse grass, my life that broken teacup,
      that bottle hurled toward

its new home, bed of shard and salt dulled
      by thousands of tides,

birthed or broken, I don't know which.
    My story is heaving something

and hearing it smash with joy, almost forgiveness.
    I did my best, I waited faithfully

for vision and held my own like the lip
    of the coke bottle in sand,

and when I came together again I was
    cracked light, vein of blue sea,

porcelain cheek, an exploded throat of grit,
    I was made of it—scarred glass,

crude, gleaming, remade.

Sunbathing

Once, when I was twenty-one, a hundred students
naked around a lake,

and in loathing I let myself be free and lay
on my towel, breasts

to the sun, swam that way, and squatted
and dried, and looked

to see whose body was better, whose worse,
whose gathered

like cotton under the skin, who sagged,
strutted, stared down.

For comfort I thought, *they're frightening,*
who love themselves,

diving, splashing, swimming up to the men,
their breasts floating.

What the sun did to my tender skin that day
I don't want to remember.

Even fish have their scales, animals fur,

not just this small arrow-shaped patch of hair
pointing toward the hidden bulb,

hollowed ground of lost Eden, where the tree waits

to respring, and the fruit

to drop at my feet.

In time I understood what I was made for.
Knew how long the bulb

could wait underground before it split
into flower,

how later it would rot and when I'd die
I'd taste the ground-up

mineral of petal and stem, the well
of mucous and blood,

and come to see I had loved this body

without knowing it, and it had loved me—

body and spirit—small, floating—
how we sometimes moved

as one, unclothed in the moist air.

All the Earth Around

That day my luck turned, it was like stepping
into one of those paintings of the *Peaceable Kingdom*,
the way she handed me the postcards I admired
and said *take them*, or how the old man fixed
my windshield wipers in five minutes refusing
my money, not knowing I drove blind for miles
through waves of rain, and how that thickening of
light, and the damp working into my bones

became beautiful, as if I could finally see through
my stained-glass eyes; and I wanted to put my cheek to
one of the paintings, or really it was only a postcard
of the painting, with an orchid in the foreground
and hummingbirds touching beaks, birds suspended
in space as if it didn't take all their strength
to stay there, then a little to their left the woven
nest, perfect eggs smaller than my eyes,

and I said, *something's changed*, I didn't mean
purple crocuses in mud or the white birch
I touched for its paper bark, but
the grove of bamboo leaning in rain,
how when those fine green bodies parted
I could see the painting waiting like a window
in the wet field, open, but without people,
the kingdom loving and hardly in need,

not even of mercy, so I might become an animal
and enter on four legs, or sprout clear wings
finding a language of touch or smell,

dragging my belly out of hiding, pink skin
exposed to sun or cold, an animal without
scales or claws, the kind usually kept out,
so when I got back in the car feeling
I'd almost touched that tulip or orchid,

almost got close to wings and wide fronds, or maybe
felt that painted world swelling toward me while
the March sky drained, I sensed a green I couldn't see,
felt it emerge from all the earth around,
wet surfaces gleaming, invisible green
beginning to coat fields and trees, then the kingdom
itself breaking free of the painting, coming
toward me, where it passed through my car,

through my body, and disappeared.

Radio

Above birch trees, the wires make the same
hum my legs make crossed over

one another, like something four-winged just outside
my ear. We're joined more by sound

than light and hardly know what we're hearing,
standing over the radio

lost in a hive of music, somewhere a Bach
variation, the cello moaning,

or a jazz singer dying on her feet, gripping
the mike, somewhere a brown

gardenia and dish towel dropped on the floor,
newspaper spread on the table.

I close my eyes unable to find the notes, trying
to play all my instruments,

breasts, throat, thighs rubbing, knowing
how hard it is to take desire

to the world, to give it away. How many times
did I start over, trying

to get it right? Like the singer on the radio.
Feel her exhaustion as she leans

on the piano saying, *Another take,*
she's giving it away, dying

faster so the notes flock my kitchen and gather
overhead. Whoever can't feel

that rising in the chest can't enter her grief
knowing just how

it's going to end. The bass player knows
and bends into his bass,

the piano player loves her always, he can't
stop. In her song

all the failures mean something, they build up
and out, held together

by the cries of instruments. When she finds
the last note it rides

toward me from a far off place, drawn out
as if she knows her worth,

who else will come from the cracks of
an old recording, saying

here is my last breath, the note lingering,
humming in the room,

following me to the sink like an autumn bee
holding out against the cold,

rolling over in the corner of the window,
still singing, even

when it's gone—

Drenched

Ocean is the first noise of wilderness, a slapping and
rolling of internal thunder or

hissing which is everywhere even under the cement of cities.
It's the drenching of the lightless that lifts

to absorb you no matter how one man learned to kick
the sharks' heads and stupefy them

or how he could swim five miles in the cold sea, swells and all,
and his title was *Rescue*; even so,

someone was always singing that same song—*Walking the
Edge*—and almost no one

heard it, not until they were drenched did it *all become clear,*
as they say, but clarity is the other side

of whatever I've tasted though I've had a drop or two
in my time and it was so sweet

so absolute I had to lose it over and over it was a drop
of water in the mind's pool and for

an instant it hovered holding perfect light then fell
and I could feel it inside me, floodlit,

and I could have that clarity for a cost, for a moment, for
blood, like seeing into the meaning of a leaf,

or of mist, the meaning of meaning, where love, as a force,
becomes inevitable, not the ruin I thought

I made, not the desolation I thought I knew but a clarity that
was there all the time, brilliant,

metallic, its taste down my back a ringing of sorts,
just a drop that ended in

the wilderness of mind and was lost like all the others.

Little Church

On Good Friday you call from across country
to describe crosses pushed

in wheelbarrows, penitents with mouths full of rocks.

Don't pray for me, is all I can think, my old faith
crawling sideways over

the dry earth, changing shapes, refusing the vinegar,
the sad sponge. I'm trying not

to plan ahead for love's daily resurrections—love born, slain,

reborn in the rumpled bed. When are you coming home?

You can't know how a woman wants, can't know
how forgiving her breasts

feel when finally found under their wrappings

as if they'd been waiting to be touched but didn't know it,
or how the muscular hand

of the vagina keeps calling, *enter, enter*, no matter
how long it takes you

to hear, how it then
lets go, cupping

the spittle and milk. Some days my belief is
a pale thing, like when

the blue afterbirth of love hangs
so heavy, the mouth of love

limp and open with weariness. The flesh knows
this one thing, it practices

for its own demise as when

giving birth, in and out of pain, a voice said, *This
is what it's like to die.*

As for the scolding bells,

I try not to listen, I'd rather feel my breath
rising toward you, so distant

from me, seeking the stray hairs at the nape
of your neck.

What horror would it take for me to go back
to the old words, to kneel again—

instead I lean into my pillow, my legs
slightly open, waiting

for when we meet skin to skin, having
to decide who I am

now that my gods have fallen away. Sometimes
only touch can help me

when I'm released with a cry

and returned to my loneliness. See how
the bed is a little church where

we have given up and taken back, spoken
in tongues, worshipped

and worshipped, then lapsed each night,

into oblivion.

Gloryland

I've got a home in Gloryland that outshines the sun
    –African-American spiritual

I thought about the dead and the myriad
as if they perched on my shoulder all the time
talking in my ear—though I can't hear them,
stuck here in the ghetto of the living. Well then, let
the comfort of Gloryland and angels like cats of different
sizes with their fierce wings and purring blow
some semblance of faith back to me. And what
of my brother, dead, who clowning
held a gun to his head and blew himself
into the nebula sac while someone cried
come back . . . where in the name of dust
has he risen, what star claims him?
Tonight, under the bare bulb, no wind through
the dusty curtain, only the memory of the woman
on the silver bus clutching packages on her lap
who turned to me and said *In the next world
I won't have to carry anything,*
and I almost added, *Or wash my hair. And my feet
will be straight again, and point forward.*
I should have said, *I want to love better.*
Or I should have turned to her so we
could rock together, shoulder to shoulder,
mute but full of the same desire to be
unburdened, redone as flint or air. And
I wanted to say what I sometimes remembered when
I was rich in remembering, how even the pitted bricks
on the buildings seemed brimming with love,
and how long it had been since I felt such things.
I wanted to tell her it was the light this side

of everything and no matter what happened
there would always be humming, a thin melody
of divine bees, rotting wood, the buzz of those
we no longer hear. Or I should have run
home and begged you to stay with me
in the city of the living, under star-ash,
under the roar of angels laughing and their
fingers long as rivers, with my bags of salt
and your eyes like trees drawing down
the light, since your name is more than
half-written and mine is traced in chalk,
and I could have told you what the dead know—
how failed I am in love, how much I've forgotten—
though I never again want to know the future
and I think it's fine if the dead stay dead no matter
how much I miss them or all I never
risked for them, and I saw my hand
lifting into air as my hand passing through
a hundred worlds at once because the dead
are better at forgiveness, and now that I live
by a river I should get wet every day,
and if I want to feel how the dead move,
I should take up rowing.

What Will You Feed Them?

Scraping corn till its milk covers
my hands. Silky pile of husks. Tomato,
rosemary, chives from the garden.
Dreaming back far into the flesh of the plant.

How we are plants grown awkward and strange.

We saw the tail hanging from the hawk's
beak as it flew off, an apple protruding
from the mouth of the deer.

I whisked and pounded, sifted
and sliced. It was mortar
for their bones. It was what
we found in the woods.
The egg that fit so well in my palm
and what came out of it.

Fire. Blood. Fungus.
Muscle. Marrow. Greens.
Nuts and garlic, wild carrot.

It's the food inside the food,
the invisible heart of the berry,
how it goes on beating
in the hallways of the body.

When the Complete comes to find me
the one question will be, *What did
you feed them?* As if I could
remember the colors arranged

just so, the balance, a lifetime
of salt thrown into the pot
and whirling there. As if each
bite was language broken
down in the mouth, each word

tasting of its sour its bitter
its sweet, to stem the craving.
What we swallowed all those years—

platter of distress, bowl
of hope. What I chewed—my own
fingers and lip. *What did you feed them?*

I fed them love. *What did you feed them?*
Love and bones, gristle,
sermons, air, mercy,

rain, ice, terror and soup, anger and dandelion
and love. *What did*

you feed them? Go to sleep
in the straw and when you wake up
I will give you something warm in a cup,

I will mix it myself, and when the Complete
finally comes for me I'll have water
hot on the stove, the tea

just right, I'll say I've sucked
the bread of this life
but I'm never full, I'll go
with my mouth open—

Polar, Dobby Gibson
Pennyweight Windows: New & Selected Poems, Donald Revell
Matadora, Sarah Gambito
In the Ghost-House Acquainted, Kevin Goodan
The Devotion Field, Claudia Keelan
Into Perfect Spheres Such Holes Are Pierced, Catherine Barnett
Goest, Cole Swensen
Night of a Thousand Blossoms, Frank X. Gaspar
Mister Goodbye Easter Island, Jon Woodward
The Devil's Garden, Adrian Matejka
The Wind, Master Cherry, the Wind, Larissa Szporluk
North True South Bright, Dan Beachy-Quick
My Mojave, Donald Revell
Granted, Mary Szybist
Sails the Wind Left Behind, Alessandra Lynch
Sea Gate, Jocelyn Emerson
An Ordinary Day, Xue Di
The Captain Lands in Paradise, Sarah Manguso
Ladder Music, Ellen Doré Watson
Self and Simulacra, Liz Waldner
Live Feed, Tom Thompson
The Chime, Cort Day
Utopic, Claudia Keelan
Pity the Bathtub Its Forced Embrace of the Human Form,
    Matthea Harvey
Isthmus, Alice Jones
The Arrival of the Future, B.H. Fairchild
The Kingdom of the Subjunctive, Suzanne Wise
Camera Lyrica, Amy Newman
How I Got Lost So Close to Home, Amy Dryansky
Zero Gravity, Eric Gamalinda
Fire & Flower, Laura Kasischke
The Groundnote, Janet Kaplan
An Ark of Sorts, Celia Gilbert
The Way Out, Lisa Sewell
The Art of the Lathe, B.H. Fairchild
Generation, Sharon Kraus

Alice James Books has been publishing exclusively poetry since 1973. One of the few presses in the country that is run collectively, the cooperative selects manuscripts for publication through both regional and national annual competitions. New regional authors become active members of the cooperative, participating in the editorial decisions of the press. The press, which historically has placed an emphasis on publishing women poets, was named for Alice James, sister of William and Henry, whose fine journal and gift for writing went unrecognized within her lifetime.

Typeset and Designed by Dede Cummings
Printed by Thomson-Shore